Abuse Among Family and Friends

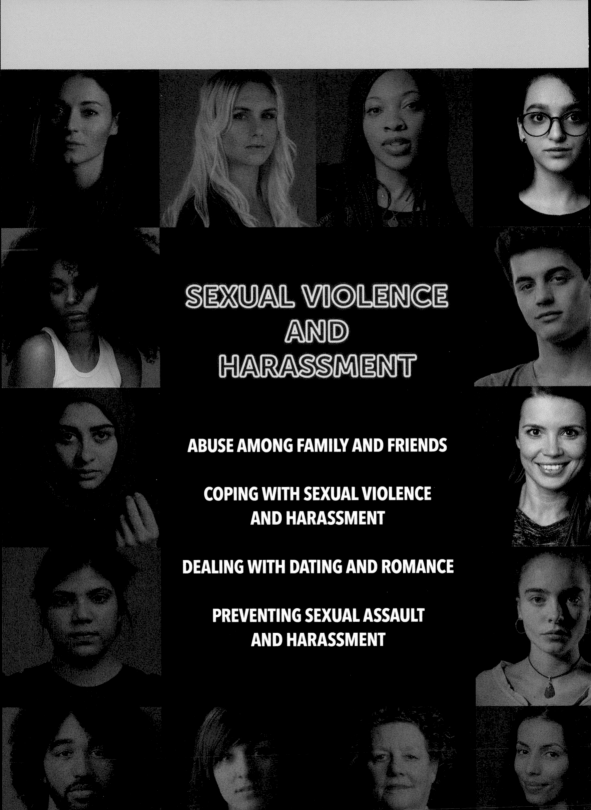

SEXUAL VIOLENCE AND HARASSMENT

ABUSE AMONG FAMILY AND FRIENDS

COPING WITH SEXUAL VIOLENCE AND HARASSMENT

DEALING WITH DATING AND ROMANCE

PREVENTING SEXUAL ASSAULT AND HARASSMENT

Abuse Among Family and Friends

Mason Crest
450 Parkway Drive, Suite D
Broomall, Pennsylvania 19008
(866) MCP-BOOK (toll-free)
www.masoncrest.com

First printing
9 8 7 6 5 4 3 2 1

ISBN (hardback) 978-1-4222-4200-1
ISBN (series) 978-1-4222-4199-8
ISBN (ebook) 978-1-4222-7606-8
Cataloging-in-Publication Data on file with the Library of Congress.

Developed and Produced by National Highlights Inc.
Editor: Peter Jaskowiak
Interior and cover design: Annemarie Redmond
Production: Michelle Luke

QR CODES AND LINKS TO THIRD-PARTY CONTENT

TABLE OF CONTENTS

KEY ICONS TO LOOK FOR:

Words to Understand: These words with their easy-to-understand definitions will increase the reader's understanding of the text, while building vocabulary skills.

Sidebars: This boxed material within the main text allows readers to build knowledge, gain insights, explore possibilities, and broaden their perspectives by weaving together additional information to provide realistic and holistic perspectives.

Educational Videos: Readers can view videos by scanning our QR codes, providing them with additional educational content to supplement the text. Examples include news coverage, moments in history, speeches, iconic sports moments, and much more!

Text-Dependent Questions: These questions send the reader back to the text for more careful attention to the evidence presented there.

Research Projects: Readers are pointed toward areas of further inquiry connected to each chapter. Suggestions are provided for projects that encourage deeper research and analysis.

Series Glossary of Key Terms: This back-of-the-book glossary contains terminology used throughout the series. Words found here increase the reader's ability to read and comprehend higher-level books and articles in this field.

SERIES INTRODUCTION

You may have heard the statistics. One in 4 girls and 1 in 6 boys are sexually abused before turning 18 years old. About 20 percent of American women are raped at some point in their lives. An online survey in 2018 found that approximately 81 percent of women have experienced some form of harassment.

Crimes like these have been happening for a very long time, but stigma surrounding these issues has largely kept them in the shadows. Recent events such as the Me Too movement, the criminal prosecutions of men like Bill Cosby and Dr. Larry Nassar, and the controversy surrounding the confirmation of Judge Brett Kavanaugh to the U.S. Supreme Court have brought media attention to sexual violence and harassment. As it often happens, increased media attention to a social problem is excellent in many ways — the availability of information can help people avoid being victimized, while also letting survivors know that they are not alone. Unfortunately, the media spotlight sometimes shines more heat than light, leaving us with even more questions than we had when we started.

Teen Dating Violence Hotline

1-866-331-9474

TTY: 1-866-331-8453

En Español: 1–800–799–7233

Text: "loveis" to 22522

That is particularly true for young people, who are just dipping their toes into the proverbial dating pool and taking their first steps into the workplace. Two volumes in this set (*Preventing Sexual Assault and Harassment* and *Coping with Sexual*

Assault and Harassment) address the "before" and "after" of those very difficult situations. The volume *Dealing with Dating* looks at romance — how to date as safely as

National Sexual Assault Hotline

1-800-656-HOPE (4673)

Online chat: https://www.rainn.org

possible, how to build emotionally healthy relationships, and what to do if something goes wrong. And finally, *Abuse among Family and Friends* takes a look at the painful issue of sexual abuse and exploitation of minors — the vast majority of whom are abused not by strangers, but by family members, acquaintances, and authority figures who are already in the young person's life. These books hope to provide a trustworthy, accessible resource for readers who have questions they might hesitate to ask in person. *What is consent really about, anyway? What do I do if I have been assaulted? How do I go on a date and not be scared? Will my past sexual abuse ruin my future relationships?* And much more.

In addition to the text, a key part of these books is the regularly appearing "Fact Check" sidebar. Each of these special features takes on common myths and misconceptions and provides the real story. Meanwhile, "Find Out More" boxes and dynamic video links are scattered throughout the book. They, along with the "Further Reading" pages at the end, encourage readers to reach out beyond the confines of these pages. There are extraordinary counselors, activists, and hotline operators all over North America who are eager to help young people with their questions and concerns. What to do about sexual violence and harassment is a vital but difficult conversation; these books aspire to be the beginning of that discussion, not the end.

INTRODUCTION

A man loiters in a dark alley with a knife in his hand, waiting for a young girl to pass by.

A man parks his filthy van alongside a playground, offering candy to persuade kids to get into the vehicle with him.

A man grabs a child who got separated from her parents at the local Walmart; before she knows what is happening, she is being sold as a sex slave in a foreign land.

These are the kinds of images many people have of sexual predators. But while it would be wrong to say these types of events never happen, they are rare. The concept of "stranger danger," which supposes that the greatest threats to children are people they've never met, is largely a myth. Depending on the survey, between 90 and 94 percent of sexual abuse is perpetrated by someone the child already knows.

An uncle or stepfather. A teacher or coach. A neighbor, a pastor, a sister's boyfriend. As uncomfortable as it is to admit, these are the true faces of sexual abuse. They take advantage of the authority (or perceived authority) they hold over children.

Sexual abuse among families and friends can happen anywhere, irrespective of race, class, or gender. Crime statistics already tell us that the abuse is common — a famous study by the Centers for Disease Control and Prevention (CDC) estimated that 1 in 4 girls and 1 in 6 boys will be sexually abused before they are 18. A more recent estimate put

the number at 1 in 10 children. Untreated traumas from sexual abuse result in higher rates of depression and anxiety, suicide, substance abuse, eating disorders, and other problems.

This book will provide the facts about child sexual abuse – what it is, how it happens, and what we can do about it. Whether you have been abused yourself or you have concerns about someone else, there will be advice and information you can use.

FACT CHECK!

Myth: *If an adult doesn't cause a child any physical pain, the sexual activity is not abusive or harmful.*

Truth: Sexual activity between an adult and a child is abuse, period. The adult in question is absolutely harming the child.

Here are a few important things you need to know right now. First and foremost, the abuse is not the victim's fault. Nothing he or she did – or did not do – caused the abuse to happen. No one deserves to be sexually abused. There is a lot of shame associated with these crimes, and while that's understandable, it's also misplaced. It is abusers who should feel ashamed, not the people they victimize.

Of course, that's all very easy to say, but it can be hard for abuse survivors to truly believe. That's why counseling is so important – a sexual abuse survivor should not have to bear the burden all alone. Read on for more information about how to get the support you need to heal.

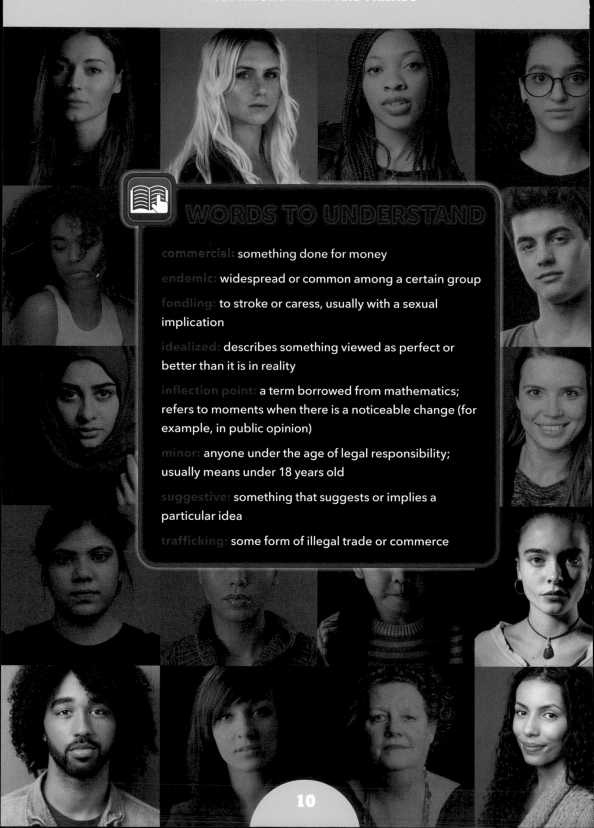

WORDS TO UNDERSTAND

commercial: something done for money

endemic: widespread or common among a certain group

fondling: to stroke or caress, usually with a sexual implication

idealized: describes something viewed as perfect or better than it is in reality

inflection point: a term borrowed from mathematics; refers to moments when there is a noticeable change (for example, in public opinion)

minor: anyone under the age of legal responsibility; usually means under 18 years old

suggestive: something that suggests or implies a particular idea

trafficking: some form of illegal trade or commerce

1

UNDERSTANDING CHILD SEXUAL ABUSE

Child abuse comes in many forms. What they all have in common is that abusers take advantage of the power imbalance between adults and kids. That's particularly disturbing when you realize that obedience to authority figures is precisely how we define a "good" or "well-behaved" child. Society expects children to "do as they're told," and meanwhile abusers exploit that fact to their own, highly damaging ends.

Physical abuse is harmful in the most obvious sense, but all forms of child abuse are damaging in less visible ways. The most important thing to remember is that the abuse is never, ever the child's fault. That may seem so obvious as to not be worth mentioning. But in fact, it's very common for abusers to say things along the lines of, "you made me do this," or "you wanted this," or "if you had done X or Y, this wouldn't have happened."

Worse still, kids often take adults at their word – assuming that, indeed, they did something to "cause" the abuse to happen. This is completely wrong. A misbehaving child, for example, has not "earned" or "asked for" mistreatment. The same goes for sexual abuse – nothing the child did or said is a justification for the adult's behavior.

WHAT IS CHILD ABUSE?

We can understand *child abuse* as referring to the mistreatment of someone under 18 by a caregiver or other authority figure. Parents and other relatives are the most obvious types of caregivers, but teachers and coaches also count, as do doctors and clergy. More informal types of "authority figures" can also be abusive, such as babysitters, camp counselors, neighbors, and family friends.

There are four main types of child abuse. Physical abuse is exactly what it sounds like – deliberately causing physical harm, whether through hitting, shoving, burning, and or any other method. In the past, hitting children to discipline them – called *corporal punishment* – was a socially acceptable parenting technique, but that's no longer true in most places. There is still disagreement about whether spanking a child rises to the level of *true*

A report of child abuse is made every 10 seconds in the United States.

POWER PLAY

A major factor in child abuse is the power imbalance between the abuser and the child. The authority that parents have over their children is pretty self-explanatory – it's even written into the law! Parents are called "legal guardians" because they are able to make a whole host of decisions on their children's behalf. Other people have various forms of power over young people, too. Teachers, coaches, and school administrators certainly do. Doctors and dentists are also authority figures in a sense. Even the 15-year-old who lives next door has more "power" than the 8-year-old she's babysitting for.

physical abuse, but child psychologists agree that there are many, far more preferable, methods of teaching children than hitting them.

The second type of abuse is emotional. Examples include verbal cruelty, humiliation, and withholding love. Every parent gets angry from time to time – after all, people make mistakes. Adults don't cease to be flawed human beings just because they're parents. But true emotional abuse involves deliberately inflicting emotional harm on a child. Refusing to help a child get necessary psychological help can also be a form of emotional abuse – if a child has anxiety issues, for instance, and the parent won't let him get treatment, that could qualify as emotional abuse.

Relatedly, neglect is the third type of child abuse. Rather than doing something wrong, neglect causes harm by not doing anything at all. Obvious forms of neglect include not feeding a child and not making sure a child is clean. Not taking a child to the doctor can also be a type of neglect, as can not making sure a child attends school. Neglect also can take subtler, more psychological forms, such as ignoring a child or allowing children to hurt themselves without stepping in.

Last but not least is sexual abuse. Any type of sexual activity with a child is sexual abuse. It's this type of abuse that we'll focus on in the rest of this book.

UNDERSTANDING CHILD SEXUAL ABUSE

The term *child sexual abuse* refers to sexual activity between an adult and a child. It can take a great many forms, ranging from rape to **fondling** to child pornography.

Any sexual activity between an adult and a child is abusive. It doesn't need to be violent to be abusive. It doesn't need to hurt to be abusive. Some perpetrators try to disguise their abuse by calling it a "relationship." An adult cannot have a romance with a child. That's not a relationship, that's sexual abuse.

Sometimes people assume that sexual abuse is just another term for rape or intercourse. According to this (incorrect) definition, if a child hasn't been physically violated in that specific way, no abuse has occurred. Others include fondling under the sexual abuse definition, but they stop there – again, wrongly assuming that some form of touching has to be involved for the behavior to qualify as sexual abuse. But, in fact, intercourse, or even touching, is not necessary for behaviors to be abusive.

NONCONTACT SEXUAL ABUSE

What's known as *noncontact* abuse can be just as traumatizing as more stereotypical types of sexual abuse. Here are some examples of sexual abusive behaviors that don't involve physical contact:

FACT CHECK!

Myth: *Rape is mainly a crime that affects adults.*

Fact: According to U.S. Justice Department statistics, 67 percent of all reported sexual assaults were against people under the age of 18; 34 percent were under age 12.

Child sexual abuse is a profound violation of the trust that children put in their caretakers.

- exhibitionism, meaning an adult exposing themselves to a child
- forcing a child to expose themselves or violating bodily privacy in any other way
- forcing a child to watch adult sexual activity (either live or filmed)
- taking or sharing sexual photos of a child
- digital interactions with a child (texts, e-mails, photos, etc.) that are sexual in nature
- masturbation in front of a **minor**

No children were touched in these examples, but they are all still abusive, illegal, and damaging to kids. It doesn't matter if it's "just" texts, "just" pictures, or "just" anything. Sexual activity with a child is abuse, period.

UNDERSTANDING CHILD SEXUAL EXPLOITATION

The **commercial** sexual exploitation of children refers to the use of children in activities such as prostitution, pornography, sex tourism, and so on. It's important to be clear on what this means: any time sexual activity is traded for something else — money, drugs, a place to sleep, anything — that is sex **trafficking**. It is, essentially, a combination of both sexual abuse and forced labor. And while it's tempting to assume that the problem exists somewhere else, in some far-off country, the sexual exploitation of children is also a problem in the United States.

Because sexual exploitation happens in the shadows, perfect data on the number of victims is basically impossible to come by. Back in 2012, the International Labour Organization (ILO) estimated that there were 4.2 million victims of global "forced" commercial sexual exploitation, generating about $99 billion in revenue. And that number doesn't include child pornography, which is even harder to quantify. In 2009 a large-scale FBI investigation of child pornography called "Operation RoundUp" found that about 21 million people tried to access child pornography online in just a two-week period.

Children and teens who are runaways or homeless tend to be at highest risk for sexual exploitation of

These days, many sex traffickers use social media to find their victims.

KNOW THE SIGNS

Kids and teens who get mixed up in sex trafficking or pornography are unlikely to talk about it – either because they are ashamed or because their abusers have manipulated them into thinking that nothing bad is happening. The National Center for Missing and Exploited Children provides families with this list of potential red flags that a child may be involved in sex trafficking:

- a history of running away from home
- traveling to other states when running away
- large amounts of cash
- several cell phones
- tattoos that suggest some form of "ownership" that the child can't explain

- sexually transmitted diseases
- signs of physical abuse
- an older boyfriend or girlfriend (especially if he or she seems controlling)
- gang involvement

Source: "Child Sex Trafficking in America: A Guide for Parents and Guardians." http://www.missingkids.com/content/dam/pdfs/NCMEC%20CST%20fact%20sheet_ParentGuardian.pdf.

all kinds. According to the National Center for Missing and Exploited Children, of the 25,000 children reported missing in 2017, about 1 in 7 was subjected to sex trafficking. In addition to finding victims on the streets, traffickers are also known to use social media to try and connect with kids to exploit. Sometimes they join social media sites and pretend to be kids themselves, hoping to befriend their victims and talk them into sexual activities.

Unfortunately, strangers on social media are far from the only threat when it comes to the sexual exploitation of children. The journal *Child Abuse & Neglect* reported that about 70 percent of children forced to participate in pornography were living at home with their families at the time. Many teens who get involved in sex trafficking are introduced to the practice by someone they know, such as a parent or foster parent, an extended family member, or a boyfriend or other peer.

SEXUAL ABUSE IN HISTORICAL PERSPECTIVE

The sexual abuse of children is as old as history itself, but it hasn't always been understood as "abuse," per se. The ancient Greeks practiced *pederasty* ("love of boys"), in which grown men had relationships with boys between the ages of 12 and 18. These relationships were often, although maybe not always, sexual. Pederasty was socially acceptable at the time; in fact, it was viewed in a positive light. People felt that it was through those mentoring relationships that the boys received a vital education about the customs of the ancient Greek elite class.

It wasn't until the 1600s in Europe that childhood slowly began to be recognized as a unique phase of life that was worthy of protection. The philosopher John Locke put forward the idea of a child as a "tabula rasa" (blank slate) who came into the world with no knowledge and needed to be gently instructed in how to think and behave. That said, the belief that children existed in a state of innocence didn't do much to stem the tide of sexual abuse. To give just one example, in New York City in the 1820s, 76 percent of rapes were committed against someone under the age of 18.

In the 1880s, patients of the psychoanalyst Sigmund Freud began telling him stories of sexual abuse (usually female patients abused by their fathers). At first Freud was reluctant to believe what he was hearing. But in time he came to not only believe the patients, he also developed "the seduction theory," which argued that the childhood trauma of sexual abuse was at the root of mental illness (then called "hysteria") in adults. Freud's peers utterly rejected this theory. The family unit was highly **idealized** at the time, so the idea that abuse within families could even exist, much less cause mental illness, was too outrageous to be believed. Freud abandoned the idea, and the seduction theory was more or less forgotten for many decades.

The phrase "child abuse" didn't enter the picture until the early 1960s, when the *Journal of the American Medical Association* published an article titled "The Battered Child Syndrome" in 1962. And it's only since the 1990s that the sexual abuse of children has been taken seriously as an important social issue.

In ancient Greek society, relationships between adult men and boys were not viewed as abusive, but they were in fact encouraged.

CHILD SEXUAL ABUSE: IMPORTANT CASES

Since the 1990s, child sexual abuse has been increasingly brought out of the shadows. There have been a number of key **inflection points** in our society's understanding of sexual abuse.

ABUSE OR OVERREACTION?

From the mid-1980s to the mid-1990s, the United States was gripped by a series of scandals about supposedly widespread sexual abuse of children in day-care centers. Some media reports even claimed that there were Satanic rituals taking place in day care that involved the abuse of children.

One very famous case involved the McMartin family, who ran a day care in Mountainview, California. When one parent reported that her child had been abused in the center, an extensive investigation was opened. Before long, 380 children were claiming that they had been abused. The school's founder, Virginia McMartin, some of her family members who worked there, and a number of other administrators were charged with hundreds of counts of child sexual abuse. The trial dragged on for years – among the longest in American history – but ultimately the McMartins were acquitted.

It turned out that the interviewers of the child accusers were overly **suggestive**, encouraging the children to say what they thought the interviewers wanted to hear, rather than the truth. Children were invited to speculate wildly on things that might have happened, as well as things that never could have. One child, for example, identified the movie actor Chuck Norris as his abuser. After the trial ended, jury members told reporters that while they did suspect the children may have been abused in some way, the

The flames of panic over child-care abuse were stoked by the large number of women who joined the workforce in the 1980s. Increasing numbers of kids in day care led to increasingly over-the-top fears about the safety of those children.

interviewing techniques were so questionable that they couldn't determine what had really happened.

The McMartin case was just one of a number of high-profile cases brought against day-care centers in this era. Analysts described the situation as a "moral panic" — a term for when a large number of people are gripped by fear of some evil that is supposedly threatening the survival of the community. The feeling of panic causes people to behave illogically, demanding actions (for instance, from the courts or police) that far exceed the actual threat.

On the more positive side, the scandals inspired a rethinking of the way children are interviewed in sexual abuse cases. Experts now understand that because children often want to please adults, they need to be asked open-ended questions that don't suggest there is a "correct" answer. Psychologists say that children rarely lie about sexual abuse, as long as they are questioned in the right way.

When Pope Francis visited Philadelphia in 2015, protesters gathered outside the cathedral where he held Mass.

THE CATHOLIC CHURCH SCANDALS

Unlike the day-care sexual abuse scandals, accusations of child sexual abuse inside the Catholic Church have turned out to be tragically real.

From Australia to Argentina, and from Ireland to the United States, it is now an inescapable fact that child sexual abuse has been (in the church's own words) "**endemic**" since at least the 1950s. Although there had been many, many rumors over the years, the dam finally burst in 2002, thanks in great part to a thorough report about sexual abuse published by the *Boston Globe*. The following year, the Archdiocese of Boston settled an $85 million lawsuit that involved 585 assault survivors.

Since then, grim revelations have kept on coming. In 2007 the Roman Catholic Archdiocese of Los Angeles settled a lawsuit brought by more than 500 survivors, for a total of $660 million; just a few months later the Roman Catholic Diocese of San Diego did the same, but with 144 survivors settling for $198.1 million. A wide-ranging 2017 report in Australia identified tens of thousands of abuse survivors in that country. In 2018 the Pennsylvania Supreme Court released findings that about 300 church officials had been involved in the abuse of more than a thousand children in that state alone.

Scandals have also occurred in Chile, Ireland, Norway, Poland, the Dominican Republic — the list goes on and on.

Not only did priests and some nuns regularly engage in child sexual abuse, but they were also protected by the church as a matter of official policy. Whenever someone in the clergy was accused of misconduct, he or she would simply be moved to a different parish, and the accusations would be hushed up. There would be no punishment of consequence to the perpetrator at all — he would just move on. And, all too often, the abuser would repeat the behavior in his next parish.

After decades of denial, the church is finally acknowledging the problem, and a number of high-ranking church leaders have resigned due to their role in covering up the abuse. In early 2018, Pope Francis penned a letter to Catholics in Chile to express his "sadness and shame" at the sexual abuse of children in that country. Millions of dollars have been paid out to survivors, and a panel has been convened to plot a course forward. But church critics still say that not enough is being done to confront the issue — particularly the problem of high-ranking church leaders covering up for the child abusers in their ranks.

SPORTS SCANDALS

Major sexual abuse scandals rocked the sports world in 2011 and 2017, the former involving a football coach, and the latter a doctor who worked with USA Gymnastics (the governing body for the sport in the United

Find out more about the Catholic Church abuse scandal.

States). As with the Catholic Church, these are in a sense double scandals —
first for the sexual abuse, and second for the cover-ups that followed.

From 1969 to 1999, Jerry Sandusky was an assistant coach for the
Penn State University football team. He also founded a charity, called the
Second Mile, which was designed to help underprivileged kids. It was
through this charity that he met and abused children, some as young as
7 years old, over the course of at least 15 years. Some of those abuses
occurred on Penn State grounds, while others occurred at his home, in his
car, and other locations. Sandusky was convicted on 48 counts of child
molestation in 2012.

But, in a sense, the real scandal was still to come. It was revealed that
Penn State administrators (including but not limited to the president of the
university) were aware of Sandusky's abuse, but took no action to stop him.
This was despite the fact that under Pennsylvania law, school administrators
are mandatory reporters, meaning that the law demands they alert
authorities to any suspicion of child abuse (see page 24 for more). Charges
were filed against a number of these administrators, some of whom were
convicted of conspiracy (the cases are under appeal as of this writing).

The scandal also destroyed the reputation of the legendary head coach
at Penn State, Joe Paterno. In the immediate wake of the scandal, Paterno
was accused of callous disregard for the well-being of Sandusky's victims.
Subsequent investigations, however, have raised questions about whether
Paterno really did know what was going on with his employee. It's worth
noting that, unlike many Penn State employees, Paterno did in fact fulfill his
basic mandatory reporting obligations — the question in the minds of critics
was whether that was enough, especially given Paterno's stature as a coach.

A similar situation has played out more recently with regard to USA
Gymnastics. The former team doctor Larry Nassar has been convicted of
multiple counts of molestation, for which he is serving more than 360 years

Olympic champion Simone Biles, one of hundreds of young women and girls who reported having been abused by their doctor, Larry Nassar.

"For years Mr. Nassar convinced me that he was the only person who could help me recover from multiple serious injuries. To me, he was like a knight in shining armor. But alas, that shine blinded me from the abuse. He betrayed my trust, took advantage of my trust and sexually abused me hundreds of times.

I was the innocent 9-year-old with a broken pelvis that was willing to trust and allow the doctor to do anything to help it feel better. I had no reason not to.

I was the 18-year-old preparing to go away to college, apprehensive and just hoping my body would be able to withstand four more years of the sport that defined my life.

Ten years of abuse and neglect. I don't like the word victim. I am a survivor, but more so, I am me."

— Alexis Moore, addressing the court at Larry Nassar's sentencing, January 2018

in prison. More than 250 women have accused Nassar of sexually abusing them when he was supposed to be providing medical treatment.

As the investigation went on, increasing numbers of Nassar's colleagues have been implicated in the cover-up. Nassar's former boss, William Strampel, not only knew about the problem with Nassar and did nothing, but he is now also facing charges of his own sexual abuse of gymnasts. Meanwhile, former coach Kathie Klages was charged in August 2018 with lying to investigators in the Nassar case. Then, in October 2018, Steve Penny, the former head of the USA Gymnastics who resigned in the wake of revelations about Nassar, was arrested and charged with evidence tampering. Allegedly, he removed files and other evidence against Nassar, with the intention of hindering an investigation into his abuses. Penny pled not guilty; as of publication, he was awaiting a trial that could end in up with 10 years in prison if he is convicted.

What's more, the sexual abuse problem in gymnastics was found to be bigger than merely one criminal in one program. In an echo of the Catholic Church scandal, an investigation by the Indianapolis Star reported that "predatory coaches were allowed to move from gym to gym, undetected by a lax system of oversight."

These scandals highlight the systemic nature of many instances of child sexual abuse. Obviously the people who sexually abuse children are the primary guilty parties, and they deserve all the punishments coming their way. But it is disheartening to consider just how many protections these abusers have received in the past – just how many people were willing to look the other way if that meant one more championship title or one more gold medal. The next frontier in the fight against child sexual abuse is likely to involve efforts to strip away the institutional protections that help keep abusers in their jobs.

TEXT-DEPENDENT QUESTIONS

1. What are the different types of child abuse?
2. What is noncontact sexual abuse?
3. What are some possible red flags of sexual exploitation?
4. What is a moral panic?
5. Regarding the USA Gymnastics scandal, why are some additional people facing legal jeopardy in addition to the abuser?

RESEARCH PROJECT

Select one of the child abuse scandals discussed in this chapter and find out more about it. Write an opinion piece about how officials responded to the crisis – did they do enough? Or, in the case of day-care scandals in the 1980s, did they in fact do too much? Where is the line, in your opinion?

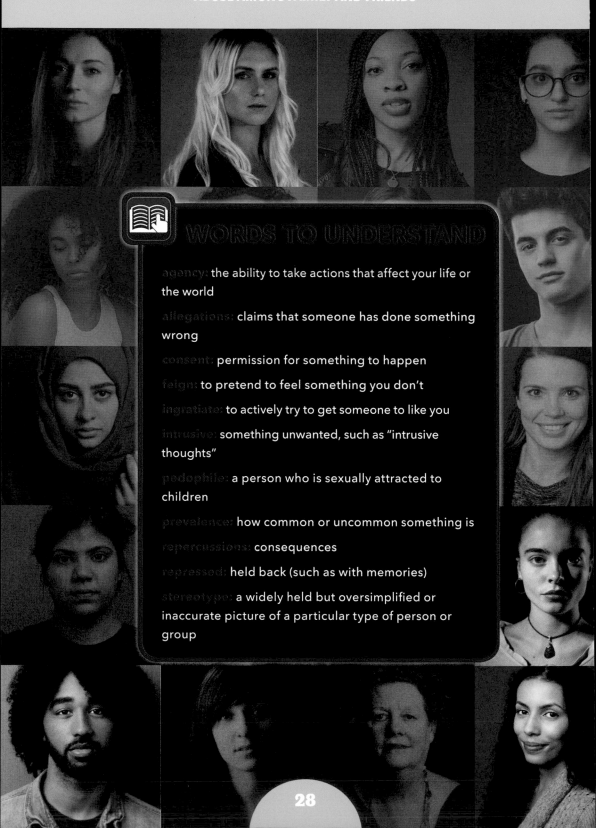

WORDS TO UNDERSTAND

agency: the ability to take actions that affect your life or the world

allegations: claims that someone has done something wrong

consent: permission for something to happen

feign: to pretend to feel something you don't

ingratiate: to actively try to get someone to like you

intrusive: something unwanted, such as "intrusive thoughts"

pedophile: a person who is sexually attracted to children

prevalence: how common or uncommon something is

repercussions: consequences

repressed: held back (such as with memories)

stereotype: a widely held but oversimplified or inaccurate picture of a particular type of person or group

2

COMMON QUESTIONS ABOUT SEXUAL ABUSE

Although child sexual abuse is a very old problem, public discussion about it is comparatively new. As a result, there is still a lot of confusion and misinformation about what child sexual abuse is, who commits it, and how we should respond to **allegations** when they arise.

In fact, one major obstacle in addressing the problem of child sexual abuse is that many people don't understand the term quite as well as they think they do. This chapter will attempt to address some of the most pressing questions and points of confusion, in hopes of gaining some clarity about what child sexual abuse is and what we should do about it.

WHO IS AN ABUSER?

There's a dangerous **stereotype** that child abusers are "dirty old men" who hang around in public parks. This is not accurate. Sexual abusers can come from all walks of life — all races, all genders, all ages.

Despite what you may have heard about "stranger danger," in reality, child sexual abuse is rarely perpetrated by strangers. According to the National Center for Juvenile Justice, only around 10 percent of child abuse is committed by strangers, while 59 percent is perpetrated by an acquaintance, and roughly 30 percent is perpetrated by a family member. Other studies place the amount of stranger abuses even lower, suggesting that only 6 or 7 percent of violations are committed by strangers.

The "old" part of "dirty old man" stereotype doesn't hold up, either. For example, among sexually abused children under the age of 6, the National Center for Juvenile Justice reports that 23 percent were abused by someone who was under the age of 18. (The percentages vary somewhat depending on the specific type of offense; see tables.)

The "male" part of the **pedophile** stereotype does have some merit — men commit the overwhelming majority of sexual assaults (roughly 96 percent). But women can also be guilty of child sexual abuse. If you look at the numbers on abused children under the age of 6, the National Center for Juvenile Justice reports that 12 percent were abused by females.

All in all, the image of the "dirty old man in the park" is highly misleading; it's even dangerous in the sense that it can distract people from risks that are statistically larger. But the notion of stranger danger lingers on, probably for a few reasons. First, even if it's "only" 6 percent of abuse cases that are committed by strangers, that's still 6 percent too many, and it's understandable to want to reduce that risk as much as possible. If that's one area that parents can do something about, we can't really fault them for trying!

TABLE 1. VICTIM–OFFENDER RELATIONSHIP IN SEXUAL ASSAULT: BY VICTIM AGE AND GENDER (IN PERCENT)

	OFFENDERS		
Age	Family member	Acquaintance	Stranger
FEMALE VICTIMS	25.7	59.5	14.7
0 to 5	51.1	45.9	3
6 to 11	43.8	51.4	4.8
12 to 17	24.3	65.7	10
MALE VICTIMS	32.8	59.8	7.3
0 to 5	42.4	54.1	3.5
6 to 11	37.7	57.7	4.6
12 to 17	23.7	68.7	7.6

Source: Howard Snyder, National Center for Juvenile Justice, "Sexual Assault Characteristics of Young Children as Reported to Law Enforcement." https://www.bjs.gov/index.cfm?ty=pbdetail&iid=1147.

TABLE 2. AGE OF SEXUAL ASSAULT OFFENDERS: BY CRIME TYPE (IN PERCENT)

OFFENDER AGE	All sexual assaults	Forcible rape	Sexual assault with object	Forcible fondling
JUVENILES	23.2	17.00	23.4	27.0
7 to 11	3.6	1.3	4.1	5.2
12 to 17	19.5	15.7	19.3	21.8
ADULTS	76.8	83.0	76.0	73.0
18 to 24	21.7	29.1	17.3	15.8
25 to 34	26.7	30.6	27.1	23.1
Above 34	28.4	23.4	32.2	34.1

Source: Howard Snyder, National Center for Juvenile Justice, "Sexual Assault Characteristics of Young Children as Reported to Law Enforcement." https://www.bjs.gov/index.cfm?ty=pbdetail&iid=1147.

On a deeper level, stranger danger speaks to the human tendency to view outsiders with suspicion, while instinctively trusting people who seem familiar. Stranger danger is comforting, in a strange way. If all we have to do to keep our children safe is teach them to avoid strangers, that seems pretty easy. It's far more difficult to figure out how to respond to threats that are, as the saying goes, coming from inside the house.

WHAT ABOUT CONSENT?

One huge misconception about sexual abuse is that if a victim doesn't actively resist the activity, that means he or she *wanted* to participate, and therefore it isn't abusive. This is totally incorrect. When it comes to young people, **consent** does not exist. Even if a child *appears* to consent, that's meaningless in the eyes of the law. The reaction of the child, whether positive or negative, is not a defense on any level.

You can see this idea reflected in the notion of *statutory rape*, which is sexual intercourse between an adult and a minor. Even if that minor appeared to consent to the activity, it's still illegal. This is because, again, people who are underage are not able to grant consent, even if they think they want to.

There are a number of very good reasons why this is so. Young children, of course, don't even know what sexual activity is. And while older kids may know what sex is in general – that is, they know "where babies come from" – that doesn't mean they understand the complex emotions that are involved or what the risks might be. Kids may simply be looking for affection and feel confused about what is happening. That's why, according to the law, adults have the responsibility to protect children from making choices or engaging in activities that can have **repercussions** they can't understand.

Further, as noted above, an older person is in a position of power over the child. Sexual abusers take advantage of the widely held belief that "good" children are the ones who follow the instructions of adults. The fact that a young person may not actively resist abuse does not mean she "wants" the activity to happen. She may just be afraid to resist, either because she's afraid of being punished or because she has been taught to "do as she's told."

Last, but not definitely not least, study after study has found that sexual abuse can do profound and long-lasting damage to children. Problems later in life can include depression, anxiety, substance abuse, and many other challenges. This is why it's so important that we protect children from abuse and exploitation by those who are more powerful.

TABLE 3. AGE OF CONSENT LAWS: BY STATE

STATE	Age of consent	Close-in-age exemption*	STATE	Age of consent	Close-in-age exemption*
Alabama	16	Yes	Montana	16	No
Alaska	16	Yes	Nebraska	16	No
Arizona	18	Yes	Nevada	16	No
Arkansas	16	Yes	New Hampshire	16	Yes
California	18	No	New Jersey	16	Yes
Colorado	17	Yes	New Mexico	17	Yes
Connecticut	16	Yes	New York	17	No
Delaware	18	Yes	North Carolina	16	Yes
District of Columbia	16	Yes	North Dakota	18	No
Florida	18	Yes	Ohio	16	Yes
Georgia	16	No	Oklahoma	16	Yes
Hawaii	16	Yes	Oregon	18	No
Idaho	18	No	Pennsylvania	16	Yes
Illinois	17	No	Rhode Island	16	Yes
Indiana	16	Yes	South Carolina	16	No
Iowa	16	Yes	South Dakota	16	No
Kansas	16	No	Tennessee	18	Yes
Kentucky	16	No	Texas	17	No
Louisiana	17	No	Utah	18	Yes
Maine	16	Yes	Vermont	16	Yes
Maryland	16	No	Virginia	18	Yes
Massachusetts	16	No	Washington	16	No
Michigan	16	No	West Virginia	16	No
Minnesota	16	No	Wisconsin	18	No
Mississippi	16	Yes	Wyoming	17	No
Missouri	17	No			

*Note: A "close-in-age exemption" refers to the idea that two partners who are close in age (for example, two high-school students) are not committing statutory rape.

Source: United States Age of Consent Map. https://www.ageofconsent.net/states.

WHAT IS GROOMING?

According to the stranger danger model of child sexual abuse, the stranger offers gifts to the child as a way of winning their trust. We now know that only a small percentage of sexual abuse cases actually play out that way. However, the idea of a "stranger with candy" is a helpful way to begin talking about grooming.

Grooming is the name for psychological manipulations that some abusers employ to win the trust of their victims. Literal gifts can definitely be part of the grooming process, but more metaphorical gifts, like compliments and undivided attention, are a part of it, too. Abusers may specifically seek out victims who appear to have low self-esteem, in the hopes that these people will be more receptive to being flattered and told how "special" they are.

Later stages of grooming involve attempts to isolate the victim from others. Isolation can happen both physically – getting the victim alone, for example – and psychologically – such as emphasizing the secretive nature of their relationship, or threatening the victim if he or she tells anyone about what's going on.

If the abuser is not a relative of the target, it's not uncommon for him to try and **ingratiate** himself with the entire family. After all, accusations of abuse from a "close family friend" are far less likely to believed. There is an element

DROPPING THE BOMB

A technique called "love bombing" was invented by cult members. It's used to manipulate people who've been targeted as potential recruits to the cult. Members overwhelm the recruit with enthusiasm, positivity, and approval, thus raising the recruit's self-esteem and implying that no one else cares about the recruit as much as the cult members do. Love bombing is itself a type of extreme grooming – it's *fake* love, feigned in order to achieve some other goal.

of con artistry to grooming: sexual abusers present one face to the family, but a very different one to the target of the abuse. They work to gradually win people over so that they can carry on with their criminal activities without suspicion.

FACT CHECK!

Myth: *Because I was friendly toward my abuser, the abuse was partially my fault, too.*

Fact: The victim of sexual abuse is not at fault, ever. Being nice to someone in a position of power is not only understandable, it's expected in most situations. Friendliness is not an invitation to sexual abuse.

Some grooming actions are hard to distinguish from simple acts of kindness, which is what makes it so difficult to notice at first. The sexual aspect of grooming also starts in very innocent-seeming ways, such as putting a hand on the target's knee or rubbing his or her back. These actions are designed to gradually get victims accustomed to the idea that touching is a "natural" part of that relationship.

Grooming is not only difficult to spot when it's happening, but it also can be hard to resist. After all, who doesn't want to be liked? Who doesn't want approval, especially of adults or older teens who seem to "have it together"? If you have been groomed by someone, try not to blame yourself. There is nothing wrong with you — you have been targeted and manipulated. People around you have been conned. Many, many adults and children have been misled by grooming techniques.

Find out more about grooming.

WHAT ARE RECOVERED MEMORIES?

Trauma has a profound effect on the human brain – particularly the part of the brain that stores memories. Many trauma survivors report having extremely vivid memories of parts of their trauma, while simultaneously having only vague recollections of other aspects. A rape survivor might clearly recall what was playing on the radio when she was attacked, but she might simultaneously have blocked out the address of the house she was in.

Memory can be particularly tricky in cases of child sexual abuse, both because of the high degree of trauma involved and because of the developing brain of the child. What's more, it's very common for years to pass between the moment when the crime happened and the moment when the survivor is able to talk about it.

The theory of **repressed** memories argues that sometimes people who have undergone severe trauma will lose the ability to remember the traumatic event. Therapy may be able to bring back, or "recover," those memories. The idea of repressed or recovered memories of child sexual abuse was very much

Although some psychologists are skeptical of recovered memories, others say they have had numerous patients "rediscover" the memory of an old trauma that had been lost.

WHAT ABOUT FALSE ACCUSATIONS?

Sometimes people who work with children, such as teachers and coaches, worry about being falsely accused of abuse by a child. Child sexual abuse is a truly horrible crime; understandably, most adults react emotionally to the idea that children could be violated in this way. A teacher who is accused of committing sexual abuse could find his or her career in ruins before any investigation is begun, much less completed.

False allegations do occur from time to time, but they are rare. Unfortunately, the exact prevalence is extremely difficult for researchers to determine. The best a wide-ranging study published in 2018 was able to conclude was that "(a) the vast majority of allegations are true but (b) false allegations do occur at some non-negligible rate." Psychologists believe that children almost never invent such accusations on their own, but rather have the ideas suggested to them by adults. That may be why false allegations appear to be a larger problem in child custody cases than in educational settings.

in vogue in the 1990s, when hundreds of adults began recovering memories of sexual trauma that had occurred long before. However, some psychologists worried that what patients thought were memories were actually just suggestions made by therapists.

Around this time, a spate of child abuse accusations against day-care providers caused a national panic (pages 20 to 21 for more on this). It turned out that many of the "memories" the children had may have been induced by the people interviewing them. Follow-up studies suggested that young children can be talked into "remembering" things that didn't happen. But what this says about repressed memories in general isn't clear — just because children tend to be open to suggestion, that does not mean that every memory they have is incorrect.

Whether or not recovered memories are real remains one of the more controversial questions in all of psychotherapy, and it has yet to be definitively resolved.

WHAT ARE THE LONG-TERM EFFECTS OF SEXUAL ABUSE?

Childhood sexual abuse can have devastating effects on survivors for a variety of reasons. The abuse is a profound violation of trust; children are told to listen to adults, and then an adult came along and took advantage. The adult also violated the child's sense of control over their own body. It's very difficult for anyone – and kids especially – to be denied the right to control what happens to them physically. The experience may cause the survivor to swing between extremes of tremendous anger at the betrayal and a crippling sense of helplessness at the loss of **agency**.

Traumatic experiences such as sexual abuse have a way of rewiring the brain. On a chemical level, people who have experienced abuse respond to stress differently than people who haven't. According to psychologists, trauma survivors can get stuck in a state of oversensitivity to stress – as though their fight-or-flight response is constantly turned on. Trauma makes our thought processes more chaotic – it becomes more difficult to "think straight," as the saying goes – and the resulting behavior can also be more chaotic.

People who have survived sexual abuse also tend to carry around a lot of shame and self-blame for what happened to them. This is completely unfair, of course, because a child is never at fault for sexual abuse. But the abuser was a respected authority figure or beloved member of the family, and it can be very difficult for the survivor to think any negative thoughts about that person. Instead, the survivor takes all the responsibility for the abuse rather than accept that the other person was in the wrong.

This shame can curdle into self-hatred. Survivors may feel "dirty," or that they are just fundamentally "wrong" or bad in some way. For that reason, survivors are at increased risk for depression, anxiety, drug or alcohol abuse, and eating disorders.

WHAT IS POST-TRAUMATIC STRESS DISORDER?

First identified in war veterans, post-traumatic stress disorder (PTSD) is a type of anxiety disorder found in people who have experienced severe trauma. Survivors of child sexual abuse are definitely at risk for PTSD, which can result in insomnia, nightmares, flashbacks, and intrusive thoughts about the experience. Outbursts of anger or irritability, feelings of worthlessness, and self-destructive behavior are also often part of PTSD. According to the American Psychiatric Association, about 3.5 percent of American adults have PTSD. Fortunately, PTSD is treatable with the help of mental health professionals.

The *Three Servicemen* Vietnam War memorial in Washington, DC. Approximately 830,000 Vietnam veterans developed PTSD after their combat experience.

AM I DOOMED?

One question that haunts many abuse survivors is whether they will ever be "normal" again. Some worry about being trapped in a life of depression, substance abuse, or toxic relationships. Others hear that some abused kids grow up to become abusers themselves, and they worry they might hurt someone.

It's true that some abuse survivors experience these problems – and yes, some do go on to abuse others. *But no one is doomed to that outcome.* It is absolutely possible for people to deal with their trauma and move on from it. People do it all the time, and if you have experienced sexual abuse, you can do it, too. It may help to talk to a counselor or therapist, or perhaps join a support group of other people who have been through similar situations. With time and help, survivors *can* recover from the things that happened to them. The abuse can't be undone, but it can be understood in such a way that it isn't determining the course of your life.

Getting support from people who have been in the same situation you are in can be incredibly helpful.

The most important thing to remember is this: *you are not bad; what happened to you was bad.* You might feel broken sometimes, or that you are completely defined by your abuse. But you don't have to feel that way forever. There is hope, and there are lots of people who want to help you. You will not forever be defined by the worst day of your life – with time, it can become one fact about you among many other, happier things. In the next chapters, we will talk about how abuse survivors can heal.

 TEXT-DEPENDENT QUESTIONS

1. Roughly what percentage of sexual abusers know their victims?
2. If someone does not actively resist sexual activity, does that mean they agree to it? Why or why not?
3. Why might an abuser use grooming techniques on the victim's family?
4. Why are abuse survivors at risk for depression?
5. What is PTSD?

 RESEARCH PROJECT

Find out more about the controversial subject of recovered memory. How do psychologists go about "looking" for memories in their patients, and how are these memories "unlocked"? Write an opinion piece that either supports or critiques the notion of recovered memories. Be sure to seek out solid evidence to support your claim and not just state what you think ought to be true.

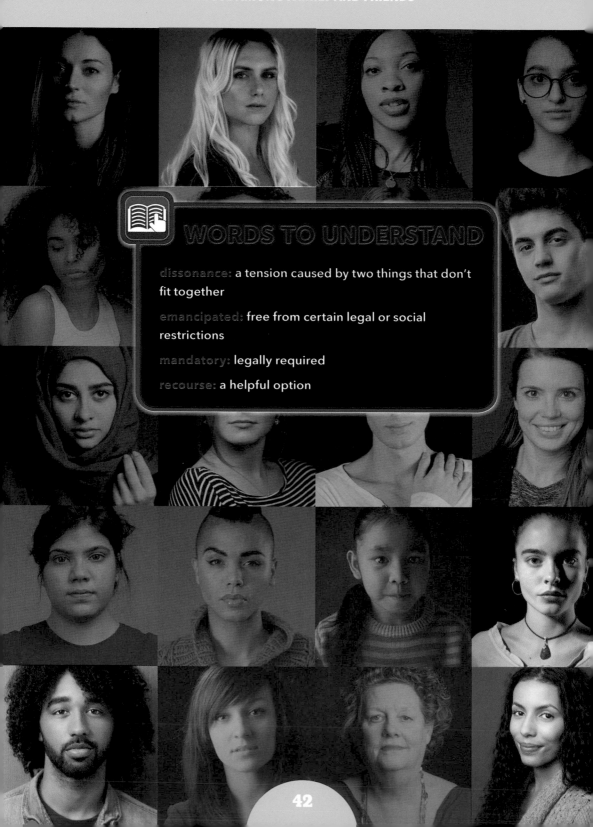

WORDS TO UNDERSTAND

dissonance: a tension caused by two things that don't fit together

emancipated: free from certain legal or social restrictions

mandatory: legally required

recourse: a helpful option

3

GETTING HELP

If you have experienced sexual abuse, you may feel that you're totally alone — that nobody could understand what you are going through. But that's not true: you are not alone. In fact, the National Association of Adult Survivors of Child Abuse estimates that there are about 42 million survivors of sexual abuse in the United States. A separate study estimated that 1 in 10 children experience some form of sexual abuse.

Of course, reading those numbers in a book is not at all the same thing as finding people who understand in real life.

As scary as it is, the only way that can really happen is for you to speak up and tell someone what happened to you. This chapter will try to help you take that step, and take away some of the mystery about what happens next.

HOW TO TELL

It can be incredibly difficult and scary to tell someone that you have been sexually abused. You may worry that you won't be believed. You may feel embarrassed — many of us find it embarrassing to talk about sex at all, much less sexual abuse. You may feel ashamed or blame yourself for "letting" it happen. You might even feel confused about whether or not what's happening is truly abuse or not. Abusers tend to be very manipulative, and they trick you into questioning your own sense of what's okay and what's not okay. Your abuser might also have told you to keep the incident secret; he might even have threatened you, saying that something bad would happen if you tell.

On top of all that, you might simply not want to say the words out loud. It's one thing to know something inside your own head; it's quite another to actually form the words and hear yourself say them. Once you take that step, things will never be quite the same again.

REASONS TO TELL

There are a whole lot of totally understandable reasons why people who have been abused may not want to talk about it. Let's focus here on the many good reasons people *should* talk about it.

- It's the first step toward making the abuse stop.
- It's the first step toward healing from the abuse.
- It may help other kids who are also being abused by this person, or who might be abused in the future.
- Keeping a secret feeds your sense that you have something to be ashamed of. You do not! Letting the secret out will help you begin to feel better.

But that is exactly why it's so important that you tell — because the abuse needs to stop. *Things should not stay the same.* And while it's comforting to think you can just pretend the abuse didn't happen, that won't make the memory go away, and it won't stop it from happening again.

If you have been sexually abused, you have been profoundly wronged by someone in your life. You should not have to carry that burden alone. By keeping the secret, you are helping to protect the person who hurt you. You don't owe that person protection; you have a right to be safe.

It takes a lot of bravery to speak out. This section looks at a few common questions people have about reporting abuse.

FACT CHECK!

Myth: *If abuse happened to you a long time ago, it's too late to do anything about it.*

Fact: It's never too late to face trauma from your past. Whether or not people in law enforcement can do anything to punish your abuser is a separate question — that depends on what happened, how long ago it was, and what the laws are in your state. But certainly trauma survivors can always benefit from speaking up and getting the help they need.

WHEN SHOULD I TELL?

This question is easy: as soon as possible. It is never too early to report a situation that makes you uncomfortable. In other words, if an adult is behaving in a way that makes you feel weird, or if you feel like you recognize some of the "grooming" behaviors mentioned on pages 34 and 35, let someone know about it. Don't think, "Oh, this isn't that bad." If an adult is making you uncomfortable, that's bad — so trust your instincts and say something. And if it turns out to be a big misunderstanding, talking to an adult can help get the confusion resolved. After all, wouldn't an adult want to have that sort of misunderstanding cleared up? A non-abusive one definitely would. So don't be afraid to ask questions or raise concerns if something makes you uncomfortable.

It is also never too late to tell. Very few kids who've been sexually abused come forward right away. It can take months, years, or even decades before some survivors are able to talk about it. That's okay. The moment you are ready is the exact right moment.

WHO SHOULD I TELL?

This question is a bit trickier for a book to answer, because everybody's situation is different. Ideally, you should talk to an adult you trust and feel close to.

The temptation, of course, is to simply say, "Tell your parents!" And that would certainly be the ideal choice. Your parents love you, and it's their job to take care of you. Now, you may worry about upsetting your parents with this news. This is understandable: it's likely that parents will, indeed, be upset to hear that their child has been abused. Here's the thing to remember, though: deep down, parents would rather hear about the upsetting thing, so they can stop it, than not hear about it and never stop it. It may be hard at first, but your parents will want to help you and make sure that the abuse ends.

You also may feel ashamed about "letting your parents down." But you didn't let anyone down! You are the victim of a terrible crime. It is not your job to protect your parents or spare their feelings. It's their job to protect you.

All that being said, telling your parents may not work in every situation. If your abuser is a family member or a close family friend, it might just be too hard for you to do. You might fear they would never believe that "Uncle John" or "Aunt Jane" is being abusive. If that's the case, there are lots of other people you can choose to tell: a different family member, teacher, school nurse, coach, doctor, or church leader are all potentially good choices. It depends on who makes you feel the most comfortable.

Favorite teachers can be great to talk to about these issues. They aren't members of your family, which means they may be less emotional than, say, parents would be.

Many teenagers opt to talk to a friend from school rather than an adult. Telling a friend your own age can be a great first step. Kids your own age are super important for helping you heal and start to feel better, and they will be key parts of your support system going forward. However, talking to a friend is not a substitute for reporting the abuse in a more formal way. Ultimately, you will need to bring your problem to an adult. Your friends aren't going to be able to take action the way adults can.

If there's no adult in your life who fits the bill, or if you simply want to practice talking about it, there are a number of anonymous hotlines that you could contact (pages 50 to 51). The hotlines are answered by trained operators who will talk to you about the specifics of your situation and help you figure out what to do next. It's important to remember that these hotlines will not force you into any particular decision. Instead, they will listen to what you have to say and provide advice about how to get the help you need.

WHAT DO I SAY?

Make sure that you and the person you're going to tell are in a private place where you won't have a lot of interruptions. You can say, "I need to tell you something important." You can also say, "This is scary for me to talk about."

When you have to explain about the abuse itself, it's okay to start slowly or to be a bit vague at first. Saying "[Someone] touched me," is a perfectly fine way to begin a conversation. Talk about how the abuse made you feel — upset, ashamed, angry, or all those things and more. You don't have to explain every single detail if you're not ready.

Take your time. Remember to breathe. If you cry, that's okay; if you don't, that's okay, too. You can take a break if you need to, and you can have several conversations over time if you want. There is no one way to do this.

Survivors share their stories of sexual abuse.

WHAT IS A MANDATORY REPORTER?

People with certain types of jobs are required by law to report child abuse to authorities; these people are called mandatory reporters. Laws about mandatory reporting are set by state governments, and they vary from state to state. In general, teachers, doctors, and mental health professionals are all mandatory reporters. In more than half of U.S. states, even members of the clergy are required by law to report child abuse. This issue is taken so seriously that states can impose fines or even jail time on a mandatory reporter who knows of but does not report child abuse.

WHAT HAPPENS NEXT?

This is the toughest question for this book to answer, because what happens next depends on who you told and how that person reacted. If you told someone who is a mandatory reporter (see box), that person is obligated to inform authorities about what you've said. You may be asked to speak to a police officer or a social services worker who is called in to investigate your case. You also may speak to a counselor about your experiences.

It can be very intimidating to talk to a stranger about these intimate issues. Try to keep in mind that counselors and therapists have special training in problems exactly like yours. You will not shock a therapist with your story. Be honest and listen carefully to the advice the counselor offers; it's his or her job to help you feel better. Therapists and counselors can help you understand what happened to you, and they can help you untangle all the complicated emotions you're having. Something that's really great about a therapist is that you can say anything you need to, without worrying about upsetting them or hurting their feelings.

HOTLINES AND RESOURCES

The groups listed here specialize in helping people who have been affected by sexual violence, child abuse, and more. They are there to listen, offer advice, and connect you to local resources in your community. They are not mandatory reporters, and they will not force you into any particular action.

RAINN

The Rape, Abuse, & Incest National Network (RAINN) is the largest anti-sexual violence group in the United States. RAINN has partnerships with more than 1,000 service providers across the country; they can help connect you with local services.

Hotline: 1-800-656-HOPE (4673)

Website: www.rainn.org

Online chat: hotline.rainn.org/online

National Child Abuse Hotline

The anti-abuse group Childhelp maintains this hotline for anyone who needs help with any type of child abuse, sexual, or otherwise. The website offers resources for kids, parents, and teachers.

Hotline: 1-800-4-A-CHILD (422-4253)

Website: www.childhelp.org

Text: CHILDHELP to 847411

National Domestic Violence Hotline

This hotline is primarily focused on helping people who are experiencing violence in their intimate relationships, including sexual abuse.

Hotline: 1-800-799-7233

Hotline (TTY): 1-800-787-3224

Website (offers chat): www.thehotline.org

National Human Trafficking Hotline

A nonprofit organization founded in 2007 to help fight human trafficking in the United States.

Hotline: 1-888-373-7888

Text: 233733

Email: help@humantraffickinghotline.org

Chat: humantraffickinghotline.org/chat

Website: humantraffickinghotline.org/report-trafficking

National Runaway Safeline

This group offers confidential services for runaways and their families, as well as for kids who are only thinking about running away.

Hotline: 1-800-RUN-AWAY (786-2929)

Website (offers chat):
www.1800runaway.org

Email: www.1800runaway.org/
crisis-online-services

Darkness to Light

Darkness to Light is a nonprofit group devoted to preventing child sexual abuse. Although most of its work is directed to adults, it does run a free crisis hotline that is available 24/7 to answer questions.

Hotline: 1-866-FOR-LIGHT

Text: LIGHT to 741741

Website: www.d2l.org

Stop It Now!

Stop It Now! is an advocacy group fighting child sexual abuse. Its website offers a lot of resources and advice about how to prevent abuse, and the hotline provides referrals and support.

Hotline: 1-888-PREVENT

Website: www.stopitnow.org

Email: www.stopitnow.org/
webform/help-inquiry

Find out more about the RAINN hotline.

SPECIAL ISSUES FOR MALE SURVIVORS

Although girls have a far higher risk of sexual abuse than boys do, the number of boys who have been sexually abused is significant. In one study by the CDC, 16 percent of the men interviewed had been sexually abused before the age of 18. Another oft-quoted study puts the overall total of men who've been sexually abused at some point in their lives at 1 in 6. (Statistics vary for a number of reasons, such as the way the questions are posed, the time frame being studied, and how sexual abuse is defined.)

Many of the emotions felt by sexual abuse survivors are the same for men and women. Anger, shame, betrayal . . . these are not gender-dependent reactions. But there are a few aspects of being a male survivor that are different from female survivors.

MASCULINITY

People in the Western world still tend to define masculinity in some pretty traditional ways. Our ideas about masculinity include things like aggression, power, toughness, and dominance. Men are not expected to express a lot of emotion (or even *have* a lot of emotion!). Vulnerability is considered to

"We tell men don't cry, don't show your emotions unless it's anger, be strong, don't ask for help, don't be vulnerable, be sexually aggressive, put work before relationships, put success before relationships. Basically we tell them that power and having power is central to being a man."

— Dan Griffin, mental health specialist

Traditional notions of masculinity don't leave a lot of room for being vulnerable.

be a "bad look" for men. And one adjective that is *not* compatible with our definition of masculinity is "victim."

Many of the immediate impacts of abuse (such as grief, fear, loss of physical control) run directly counter to our notions of what masculinity is supposed to look like. This **dissonance** can leave male survivors profoundly confused and distraught. They worry that if a "real man" is powerful and in control, a sexual abuse victim can't possibly be a real man. Male sexual abuse survivors often feel humiliated and demoralized. They blame themselves for the loss of control, when in fact nothing about what happened was under their control in the first place.

Our notions of what makes a "real man" can lead survivors to deny the truth of what happened to them. Some male survivors would rather pretend the abuse was "no big deal" rather than accept that they were victimized. In a 2015 interview, the mental health specialist Dan Griffin discussed "the guy who had sex for the first time when he was ten years old with his babysitter who thinks that's a notch on his belt. He doesn't see this as trauma, even though it is." Given our social messaging around masculinity, it's no surprise that it takes an average of 20 years for men to admit out loud that they've been sexually abused.

Instead of facing what happened, some men act out in highly masculine (hypermasculine) ways because they are trying to prove that they are "real men" despite having been abused. Unfortunately, this sometimes ends with the survivor being abusive toward others, either sexually or in other ways. If you perceive the world as divided between perpetrators on the one hand and

The term *hypermasculinity* refers to exaggerated forms of stereotypical masculine behavior.

victims on the other, there is a temptation to inflict abuse on others as a way of "proving" that you belong in the first, more masculine group, rather than in the second, weaker group. It is not inevitable that abused kids grow up to be abusers, but it does happen sometimes. That's why it's so important that boys who have been abused get help to come to terms with what happened.

FACT CHECK!

Myth: *A teen boy who has sex with an older woman should feel lucky.*

Fact: The situation is sexually abusive and can still be damaging and upsetting. A teen boy is not obligated to feel like he hit the jackpot by being sexually abused.

Being sexually abused does not mean you are weak or "not a man." Having emotions about the abuse does not make you weak, either. Somebody committed a crime against you, and *that person* is in the wrong, not you.

SEXUALITY

Because this particular type of abuse is sexual in nature, surviving it can leave boys and men with a lot of questions about their own sexuality.

The vast majority of sexual abuse – whether against boys or girls – is perpetrated by men. Consequently, some male survivors worry that being abused by a man *makes* them gay. Others wonder if they were abused *because* they are gay. It's vital to understand that, at its root, *sexual abuse is really not about the sex*: it's about the power. Yes, the abuse was sexual in nature, but that fact does not in itself prove anything about the sexuality of the person who was victimized.

A boy does not become gay because a male abused him sexually. Likewise, being gay does not mean you brought sexual abuse on yourself. Those two things – the abuse and the sexuality – are not related in any way.

LEGAL EMANCIPATION

Some kids in abusive family situations wonder if there is a legal **recourse** for them to leave home and go live on their own. The answer is: maybe, kind of, it depends.

In the United States, the legal age of adulthood (called "the age of majority") is 18. Under certain circumstances, getting married or joining the military may also make you "the age of majority" before you turn 18. It is also possible to petition the court to be **emancipated**, or declared a legal adult, if you are 16 or 17. States write their own laws for how emancipation works, so the rules vary depending on where you live.

Speaking very generally, the process is as follows. You file a request with the court (which can cost $150 or more) and notify your parents or guardians. A hearing is then held before a judge, who listens to your evidence and asks questions about why you believe emancipation is necessary. If the judge finds in your favor, you are declared a legal adult with all the freedoms and responsibilities of someone 18 or over. (There are exceptions in some states: for instance, in Illinois judges can declare you emancipated in some ways but not in others.)

The good news is, your parents no longer get to make any decisions for you. The bad news is, you now have to figure everything out yourself — including where to

CHECK IT OUT!

Emancipation is a huge decision and not something you should try to figure out alone. Find an adult you trust and talk things over. You'll also need legal advice. One place to start is at the web page "Browse Family Law Lawyers Near You" (https://lawyers.findlaw.com/lawyer/practice/family-law), which provides links to attorneys that work on emancipation cases, organized by city, county, and state.

live, how to make money, what to do about your health care, and so on. As an emancipated minor, you can sign legally binding contracts, but you can also be sued, just like any adult.

Before you jump to emancipation, you might want to consider if there is any way you can improve your current living situation without going to court. For instance, perhaps there is a member of your extended family who could take you in for a short period. In most situations, emancipation can't be undone once it's declared, so you want to be absolutely sure that this is right route for you.

TEXT-DEPENDENT QUESTIONS

1. Why is it often very scary for people to come forward about sexual abuse?
2. What are some of the potential benefits of speaking out?
3. What are some examples of mandatory reporters?
4. What are some unique issues that male survivors of sexual abuse may struggle with?
5. What is legal emancipation?

RESEARCH PROJECT

Check out the websites of the groups listed on pages 50 to 51. Explore what services they offer. Who is their target audience? What are their goals? Expand on the information given in these pages to create a brochure with detailed information about what groups are available to help people who have been sexually abused. Also be aware that there are many more organizations than what could be fit on those pages – if you find other good groups, add those to your brochure, too!

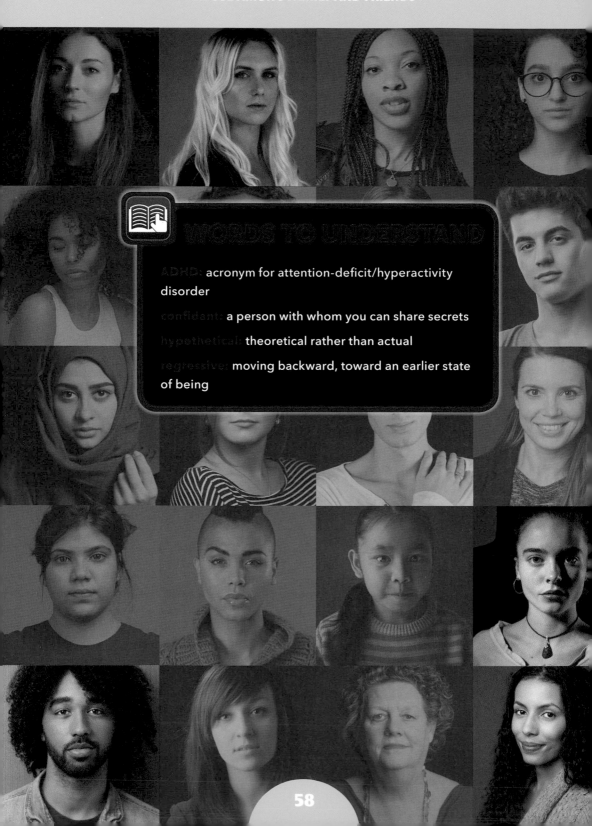

WORDS TO UNDERSTAND

ADHD: acronym for attention-deficit/hyperactivity disorder

confidant: a person with whom you can share secrets

hypothetical: theoretical rather than actual

regressive: moving backward, toward an earlier state of being

4

HELPING OTHERS

Do you know anybody with asthma? How about **ADHD**? Chances are pretty good that you know someone with one of these conditions. Unfortunately, chances are even better that, whether you're aware of it or not, you know somebody who has experienced sexual abuse. As mentioned in Chapter 1, the rates of people who have survived sexual abuse are higher than those diagnosed with either asthma or ADHD.

In this chapter we'll look at how you might be able to help someone who has experienced or is experiencing sexual abuse. Of course, it's important that you be realistic about your role. You aren't a doctor or a therapist, nor are you a police officer, so clearly there are limits to how much you'll be able to do for that person. But you can still be a good friend, and for people who are suffering from trauma, a good friend can make a big difference.

WARNING SIGNS OF SEXUAL ABUSE

It is extremely difficult for sexually abused kids to talk about what happened to them. Very young children may not have the language to even begin to explain. And even older kids hesitate to talk about it — they may feel ashamed, or they may fear being punished for making the situation even worse. But even when kids won't or can't talk about what happened in a direct way, certain behaviors may be hints that there is an underlying problem.

REGRESSIVE BEHAVIORS

Regressive behaviors are when kids don't "act their age," but instead engage in actions that are more appropriate for much younger kids. Bed-wetting, thumb-sucking, temper tantrums, and overly clingy behavior are common regressive behaviors. Trauma causes a sort of reorganization of the brain, and people who have been sexually abused may essentially get "stuck" at whatever age they were when the abuse happens. In times of extreme stress, they may go back to acting that age. For instance, a 13-year-old who was sexually abused at age 5 may have screaming temper tantrums that seem "too babyish" for a typical 13-year-old. But for her, it's a gesture back to the time when she was originally traumatized.

INAPPROPRIATE SEXUAL BEHAVIORS

It's also not uncommon for kids who have been sexually abused to act in overly sexualized ways, such as playing with toys in sexual ways, touching others inappropriately, or exposing their private parts in public.

These behaviors occur for a few reasons. First, the child may be confused about the abuse and may repeat the behaviors as a way of trying to "work out" what's happening. Also, the child may want to report the abuse but be afraid to speak up or unsure about how to do it. The sexual behavior may be an awkward sort of hint — a way of bringing up the topic and seeing how adults react. A very young child may not even know the right words to say, so she might try to demonstrate it with her toys or her own actions. Another issue is that the abuse may have created a link in the child's mind between affection and sexuality. Overly

Older kids behaving like they are younger than they are might be a sign of abuse.

sexual behavior may be a sign that the child is confused about what is appropriate and what isn't.

It's very important to remember that children who act this way are not crazy, slutty, or sex obsessed. *These behaviors are not the child's fault.* The blame rests with the adult who violated the child's trust.

SELF-DESTRUCTIVE BEHAVIORS

Teen sexual abuse survivors may act out by using alcohol or drugs, cutting themselves, developing anorexia or bulimia, skipping school, stealing, or engaging in unsafe sexual activity. These self-harming behaviors may happen regardless of whether the abuse occurred recently or in the past. In other words, the behaviors may hint at sexual abuse recently or they could be inspired by something that happened a long time ago.

Self-destructive behaviors can be worrying and frustrating to both family and friends. But sometimes parents and other authority figures focus too much on stopping the behaviors themselves, rather than looking at the underlying trauma that may be inspiring the behavior. Sometimes these behaviors are actually a message – the teen is trying to tell you that something larger is wrong.

Karen Kay Imagawa, MD.
Dir. Center Cares

Behavioral Signs of Abuse

Find out more about signs that a child may have been abused.

OTHER RED FLAGS

Here are some additional behaviors that counselors often view as "red flags" that there may be a sexual abuse issue. (It's important to note that none of these behaviors definitely means someone has been abused; these are just potential red flags. There may be some other explanation for the behavior.)

- Nightmares
- Refusal to sleep
- Insisting on sleeping fully clothed
- Suddenly not wanting to visit a place they used to like
- Sudden appearance of gifts or money with no clear source
- Sudden fear of a particular family member
- Sores around the mouth

- Abrupt appetite changes
- Difficulty swallowing
- Excessive crying
- Incontinence
- Urinary tract infections
- Difficulty walking or sitting
- Watchfulness (as though something bad is about to happen)
- Strong body odor

HOW TO BE TOLD

When young children are sexually abused, the person they are most likely to tell is a parent or other caregiver. But among teens, that's not true – the person sexually abused teens are mostly likely to tell is a friend their own age. So let's imagine that your best friend confides to you that she's been sexually abused by her stepfather. How do you react? What do you tell her?

This is a very tough moment for any friend. You are likely feeling a lot of different things at once: scared for her, angry at her stepfather, confused about why this would happen, and probably a little freaked out to be talking about this topic at all. That's natural – nobody wants to think about this stuff. But if you do end up in a situation where someone you care about discloses abuse, here are some things to keep in mind.

Remember: This conversation is a gift. In the moment when you get news like this, it may not feel like anything *good* is happening. But if you take a broad view, you'll realize that your friend is actually demonstrating how much she loves and trusts you. No one confides information about sexual abuse to someone they don't care about. It's a big deal that your friend chose you as the person she wants to talk to – it says a lot about your relationship. It's also a compliment, because clearly your friend believes that you are up to the job of helping her, or she wouldn't have brought it up at all.

Stay calm and neutral. Your friend is going to be watching your reaction very carefully. She's probably nervous about making this disclosure; any sign from you that this is a bad or unwelcome topic may cause her to shut down. Talking about sexual abuse can be incredibly awkward and uncomfortable. Try your best to avoid a tone of voice or facial expression that might suggest you think what your friend is saying is icky or weird.

Remember some key phrases. The two most important things you can say to a sexual abuse survivor are "I believe you" and "It's not your fault." Those two very simple sentences will mean the world to your friend. "It's good that you told me" is also helpful; people who have experienced sexual abuse often feel scared that no one will listen, or they feel guilty for "burdening" other people with their problem. Other phrases you can use if you get stuck are "Tell me more" and "How did you feel?" These can open the door for your friend to keep talking without pressuring her to say anything in particular.

Follow her lead. Sexual abuse makes the victim feel powerless; her control of the most private part of herself has been taken away. As her trusted **confidant**, your job is to give her back as much control as you can. Resist the urge to pepper her with questions about what happened. Instead, let her explain it at her own pace.

A NOTE ABOUT PRONOUNS

Sexual abuse can happen to anyone, regardless of gender presentation. This section uses the female pronoun for two reasons: first, because statistically speaking, far more females are abused than males; and second, because constantly saying "he or she" is difficult to read and may be confusing.

Please know that just because the hypothetical survivor on these pages is referred to as "she," in truth the survivor can be of any gender, and the advice here still applies.

Avoid judgements. If you do ask questions, make sure those questions aren't phrased as accusations. For example, "Why didn't you fight back?" is not a good question to ask, because it implies that your friend is at fault for not stopping the abuse. Instead you could ask, "How did you feel when that happened?"

Show affection . . . respectfully. If you and your friend have the kind of relationship where you hug each other, you should definitely hug your

The most important thing you can say to a friend in this situation is, "I believe you."

friend now. But first, it's a good idea to ask, "Can I give you a hug?" Your friend's sense of control over her own body has been taken away by her abuser. Asking if it's okay to hug her is just a small way of showing that you respect her right to decide who touches her when.

Seek help. Teens who are being sexually abused are afraid to report it for a wide variety of reasons: some feel deeply ashamed; some have been threatened with punishment if they tell; some are afraid of upsetting their parents; and some are afraid they'll be taken out of their home or that the adult could end up in jail. There are a lot of reasons why survivors hesitate to report, and it's important to understand that those reasons are not silly or crazy. They are real, legitimate feelings and fears.

The fact that your friend is reaching out to you suggests she might be ready to take the next step and report the abuse to an authority. If so, you should support that decision. People you might consider telling include a parent, teacher, school nurse, coach, clergy member, or counselor. Offer to go along with her if she would like, so you can provide emotional support.

That said, it's also possible that your friend is not ready to tell anyone besides you. Don't put a ton of pressure on your friend when it comes to this. Suggest that she talk to an adult, but be understanding about why she might be afraid. Consider offering those hotlines mentioned on pages 50 to 51. Hotlines can be a great first step toward reporting abuse in a more official way.

However, here's the tough part: even though your friend may not want to disclose to anyone else, you still need to tell an adult. Every situation is different, so you'll need to assess and figure out whether to go to your own parents, a teacher, or some other person. But you should not keep the information to yourself — and yes, that's true even if your friend swore you to secrecy.

SUPPORT CHANGES LIVES

It can be uncomfortable to talk to a friend about sexual abuse. You may worry about saying the "right" or "wrong" thing. But in the end, as long as you are kind and supportive, you can't go very far wrong. Several studies have found that kids who received positive support when they opened up about their abuse had fewer traumatic symptoms over the long term than those who were not supported or believed. Your kindness to your friend can help change her life, and what could be better than that?

This may be a hard thing to hear, because of course you don't want to betray your friend's trust. But this secret is just too big for you to keep. The abuse is not going to stop on its own — the only way it's going to get better is with some form of outside intervention. Keeping her secret is not going to get your friend where she needs to go. She may not see it this way currently, but you should have faith that she will understand later on, when the abuse has been stopped and she is beginning to heal. Even if you're both well into your teens, your friend is still fundamentally a kid, and so are you! This is not the sort of thing you should try and handle alone.

WHAT IS THE INVISIBLE SUITCASE?

The "invisible suitcase" is a metaphor that's used by people who work in the foster care system, and it's also sometimes employed by counselors and therapists. If you're reading this book, chances are you are neither a therapist nor a foster parent! But if you have a friend or family member who is struggling with a traumatic experience, having a basic understanding of the invisible suitcase may help you better understand what's going on inside the person you care about.

The metaphor of the invisible suitcase initially sprang from the idea of a child arriving at a foster home with all his belongings in tow. The child brings his actual luggage, but he also has an additional suitcase that nobody can see. That "suitcase" contains things like:

- memories of past traumatic experiences
- feelings inspired by those experiences (fear, shame, anger, and so on)
- feelings about himself (often negative, such as feeling worthless or that the trauma was deserved)
- beliefs or assumptions about how the world works (it is a scary place, adults are untrustworthy, and so on)

These invisible "belongings" are going to influence his relationship with his new foster family, school, and everything he encounters. If his previous experiences have been negative, it's natural for the child to assume that the new situation is going to turn out badly as well. This is sometimes called *reenactment*, which is the tendency to recreate old relationships with new people we meet.

That – combined with all the stored-up anger and fear in the suitcase – can inspire a traumatized child to act out, pushing away people such as the new foster family. That can be very frustrating for all these new folks – who, after all,

WHAT IS TRAUMA-INFORMED CARE?

Trauma is defined as an extreme event (or series of events) that overwhelms a person's ability to cope. Sexual abuse absolutely qualifies as such an event.

The term *trauma-informed care* refers to a set of ideas and practices about how to help people – particularly kids, but not only kids – who have survived these kinds of devastating events. The goal of trauma-informed care is to take survivors' experiences into account when interacting with them. The goal is to create an atmosphere of safety and acceptance, so that the survivor can begin to heal.

The principles of trauma-informed care were developed by and mainly apply to doctors, counselors, and other caregivers. In some states foster parents also get trained in trauma-informed care, too.

have no way of knowing what's in that suitcase. Unfortunately, their frustrated reactions can confirm to the child he was right ("See, I knew this wouldn't work out."). This in turn makes him more upset, and the cycle continues. In order to break the cycle, the invisible suitcase has to be acknowledged and "unpacked," so that all those negative emotions and expectations can be

addressed. You can't expect a traumatized person to not have bad feelings – having those feelings is totally normal. But it's important to acknowledge that they exist.

A therapist can help you unpack that "suitcase," to better understand how trauma in the past may be affecting your thoughts and actions today.

What does all this mean to you, as the friend or relative of a traumatized person? For one thing, it may help you to understand that people who have experienced trauma have a whole collection of complicated emotions that influence the way they react to the rest of the world. For example, a person who has survived sexual abuse may have a strongly negative reaction to being touched without permission. Getting upset about such a small thing might seem odd to you, but that's just because you haven't had the experiences that the other person has.

If your friend is acting in ways that are confusing or upsetting, remember that invisible suitcase. Maybe he is carrying something inside that needs to be brought out in the open so that it can be dealt with in a healthy way.

TEXT-DEPENDENT QUESTIONS

1. What are regressive behaviors?
2. What are some red flags that someone may be experiencing sexual abuse?
3. What are the two most important things you can say to someone who has been sexually abused?
4. How might the "invisible suitcase" impact how someone behaves?
5. What is trauma-informed care?

RESEARCH PROJECT

Find out more about the best ways to react and the best things to say when someone discloses sexual abuse to you. Write a short story or script in which a character tells a friend about an incident that happened to them. Try to put yourself in the shoes of both characters, imagining how it would feel to be in each person's position.

SERIES GLOSSARY OF KEY TERMS

adjudicated: when a problem is addressed in a formal setting, such as a courtroom

advocacy: championing or arguing for a particular thing

agency: the ability to take actions that affect your life or the world

allegations: claims that someone has done something wrong

amorphous: something with a vaguely defined shape

assess: evaluate

cisgender: describes a person whose gender identity matches that person's biological sex

coercion: forcing someone to do something they don't want to do

cognitive: relates to how a person thinks

complainant: legal term for someone who brings a case against another person

conflict resolution: a process through which people with disagreements can work together to solve them

consent: agreement or permission

corroborating: something that confirms a claim is true

credible: believable

demographic: relates to the different types of people in a society; age, race, and gender are examples of demographic categories

deterrent: something that discourages a particular activity

diagnosable: a health condition with specific symptoms and treatments that can be identified by a health-care professional

disordered: random; without a system

dissonance: a tension caused by two things that don't fit together

emancipated: free from certain legal or social restrictions

endemic: widespread or common among a certain group

entitlement: the sense that one has the right to something

exonerated: cleared of guilt

feign: to pretend to feel something you don't

felony: a category of serious crime; felony crimes come in several degrees, with "first degree" being the most serious, "second degree" being slightly less serious, and so on

fondling: to stroke or caress, usually with a sexual implication

idealized: describes something viewed as perfect, or better than it is in reality

incapacitated: describes the condition of being unable to respond, move, or understand

inflection point: a term borrowed from mathematics; refers to moments when there is a noticeable change (for example in public opinion)

ingratiate: to actively try to get someone to like you

internalize: to take in an idea or belief as your own

intrusive: describes something unwanted, such as "intrusive thoughts"

involuntary: a situation where you have no choice

LGBTQ: acronym for lesbian, gay, bisexual, transgender, and queer/questioning

mandatory: legally required

minor: anyone under the age of legal responsibility; usually means under 18 years old

nonconsensual: describes an act (often sexual) that one participant did not agree to

nontraditional: different from a widely accepted norm

norms: standards of what's considered typical or "normal" for a particular group or situation

nuanced: describes something that is complex; not "black and white"

nurturing: describes something that is supportive and warm

ostracized: shunned, shut out

pernicious: describes something that's very harmful but in a subtle way

pervasive: widespread

prophylactic: preventative

psychosis: mental impairment so severe the person loses connection with reality

PTSD: an acronym for post-traumatic stress disorder, a serious psychological condition caused by profoundly disturbing experiences

regressive: moving backwards, toward an earlier state of being

remorse: regret

repercussions: consequences

resilience: the ability to recover from difficulties

retaliation: revenge or punishment

self-determination: the ability to make your own decisions and follow through with them

sociopath: someone with a severe mental disorder who lacks empathy or conscience

spectrum: a range

STDs: acronym for sexually transmitted diseases

stereotype: a widely held but oversimplified or inaccurate picture of a particular type of person or group

suggestive: describes something that suggests or implies a particular idea

surveillance: observation; spying

trafficking: describes some form of illegal trade or commerce

unambiguous: very clear; not open to interpretation

FURTHER READING AND INTERNET RESOURCES

BOOKS AND ARTICLES

Beckett, Helen and Jenny Pearce, eds. *Understanding and Responding to Child Sexual Exploitation.* New York: Routledge, 2017.

Feuereisen, Patti. "Some Teen Girls Never Tell." *Ms. Magazine* blog, September 24, 2018. http://msmagazine.com/blog/2018/09/24/teen-girls-never-tell.

Lew, Mike. *Victims No Longer: The Classic Guide for Men Recovering from Child Sexual Abuse.* 2nd ed. New York: Quill, 2004.

NSPCC. "Grooming: What It Is, Signs, and How to Protect Children." https://www.nspcc.org.uk/preventing-abuse/child-abuse-and-neglect/grooming/.

Papisova, Vera. "Sexual Assault Survivors Write Messages They Wish They'd Received." *Teen Vogue,* April 20, 2018. https://www.teenvogue.com/gallery/sexual-assault-survivors-handwritten-messages.

Stern, Robin. *The Gaslight Effect: How to Spot and Survive the Hidden Manipulation Others Use to Control Your Life.* Foreword by Naomi Wolf. 2nd ed. New York: Harmony Books, 2018.

Townsend, Catherine, and Alyssa A. Rheingold. "Estimating a Child Sexual Abuse Prevalence Rate for Practitioners: A Review of Child Sexual Abuse Prevalence Studies." Charleston, SC: Darkness to Light, 2013. https://www.d2l.org/wp-content/uploads/2017/02/PREVALENCE-RATE-WHITE-PAPER-D2L.pdf.

WEBSITES

National Child Traumatic Stress Network (NCTSN). "Sexual Abuse." https://www.nctsn.org/what-is-child-trauma/trauma-types/sexual-abuse
The National Child Traumatic Stress Network offers comprehensive information about the effects of child sexual abuse and how the resulting trauma can be treated.

National Human Trafficking Hotline.

    https://humantraffickinghotline.org

    Funded by the U.S. Department of Health and Human Services, this site offers a wide range of resources on the issue of human trafficking, both sex trafficking and other kinds.

RAINN. "Child Sexual Abuse."

    https://www.rainn.org/articles/child-sexual-abuse

    RAINN (Rape, Abuse, & Incest National Network) offers many resources to help survivors of sexual violence, including child sexual abuse.

Stop It Now!

    https://www.stopitnow.org

    This advocacy group's website offers lots of information on fighting child sexual abuse.

EDUCATIONAL VIDEOS

Chapter 1

    Find out more about the Catholic Church abuse scandal.

    http://x-qr.net/1Jz0

Chapter 2

    Find out more about grooming.

    http://x-qr.net/1Lqm

Chapter 3

    Survivors share their stories of sexual abuse.

    http://x-qr.net/1LPN

    Find out more about the RAINN hotline.

    http://x-qr.net/1JP3

Chapter 4

    Find out more about signs that a child may have been abused.

    http://x-qr.net/1M3k

INDEX

AUTHOR'S BIOGRAPHY

H.W. Poole is a writer of books for young people, including *The Big World of Fun Facts* (Lonely Planet Kids) and the sets *Childhood Fears and Anxieties, Families Today*, and *Mental Illnesses and Disorders* (Mason Crest). She created the *Horrors of History* series (Charlesbridge) and the Ecosystems series (Facts On File). She was coauthor and editor of *The History of the Internet* (ABC-CLIO), which won the 2000 American Library Association RUSA award.

PHOTO CREDITS